U.S.A. TRAVEL GUIDES

NEVADA

BY ANN HEINRICHS • ILLUSTRATED BY MATT KANIA

The Child's World®
childsworld.com

Published by The Child's World®
1980 Lookout Drive • Mankato, MN 56003-1705
800-599-READ • www.childsworld.com

ISBN 9781503819689
LCCN 2016961181

Printing
Printed in the United States of America
PA02334

Ann Heinrichs is the author of more than 100 books for children and young adults. She has also enjoyed successful careers as a children's book editor and an advertising copywriter. Ann grew up in Fort Smith, Arkansas, and lives in Chicago, Illinois.

post card

About the Author
Ann Heinrichs

Matt Kania loves maps and, as a kid, dreamed of making them. In school he studied geography and cartography, and today he makes maps for a living. Matt's favorite thing about drawing maps is learning about the places they represent. Many of the maps he has created can be found in books, magazines, videos, Web sites, and public places.

post card

About the
Map Illustrator
Matt Kania

On the cover: Hike through Nevada's Red Rock Canyon National Conservation Area.

OUR NEVADA TRIP

Do you like adventure? Then you'll love your tour through Nevada! Just wait and see all you can do.

You'll ride out on the range with cowboys. You'll watch a gunfight in a mining town. You'll hang out with mountain men. You'll stand atop a massive dam. You'll gaze up at red rock towers. And you'll watch jackrabbits and mountain goats scampering along.

What do you think? Shall we hit the road? Then buckle up and hang on tight. We're off to see Nevada!

WELCOME TO
NEVADA

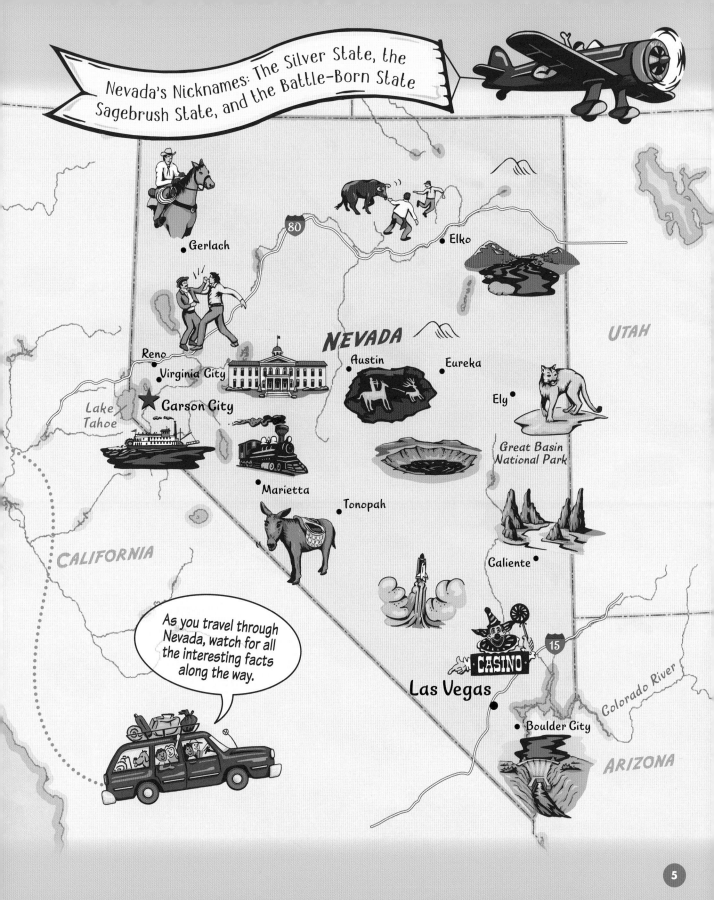

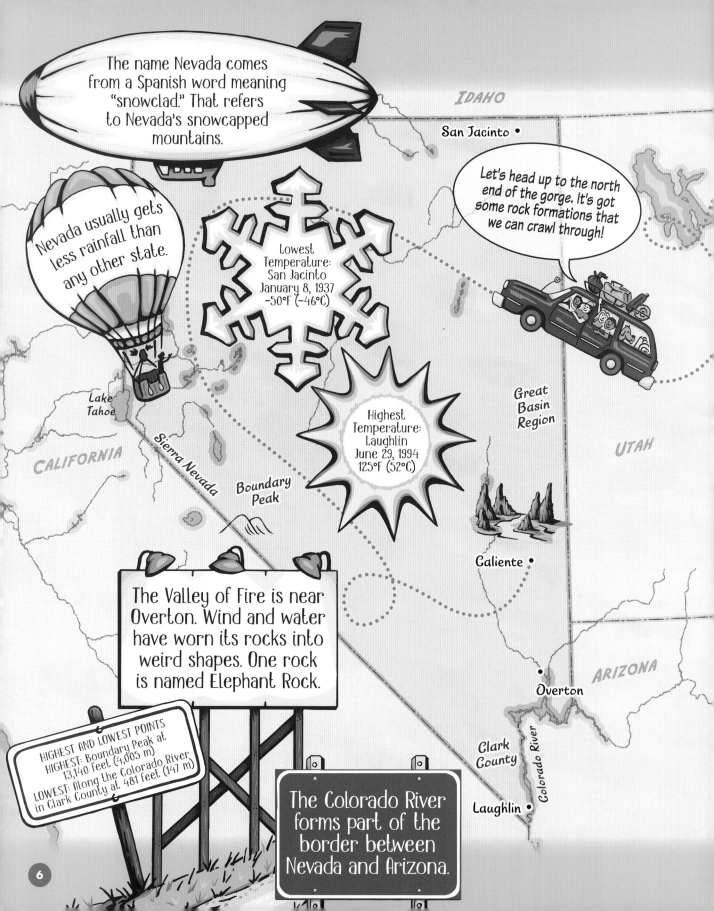

CATHEDRAL GORGE NEAR CALIENTE

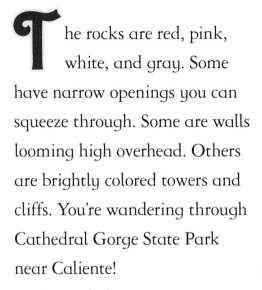

The rocks are red, pink, white, and gray. Some have narrow openings you can squeeze through. Some are walls looming high overhead. Others are brightly colored towers and cliffs. You're wandering through Cathedral Gorge State Park near Caliente!

Nevada has many areas with strange rock formations. Most of Nevada lies in the Great Basin Region. That's a dry, rugged part of the country. Flat, sandy deserts cover much of the land.

Many small mountain ranges run through the state. Swift streams rush through their rocky canyons. The Sierra Nevada are mountains on the western border. Lake Tahoe rests high in a valley there.

Check out the amazing rock formations at Cathedral Gorge!

PADDLEBOATING ON LAKE TAHOE

You're cruising around Lake Tahoe. Your boat is the *Tahoe Queen*. Its big paddle wheel turns around. That's how the boat moves through the water!

Lake Tahoe is a popular vacation spot in the Sierra Nevada. You can ride a **tram** high over the valley. In the winter, people go snowmobiling. They ski down the snow-covered slopes.

Lake Mead is another fun place. People enjoy swimming and waterskiing there. Some people like mountain climbing in Nevada. Others go hiking and look for wildlife.

Maybe you enjoy big cities. Or perhaps you prefer the outdoors. Whatever you like, you'll find it in Nevada!

Grab a kayak and cruise through Lake Tahoe's blue waters.

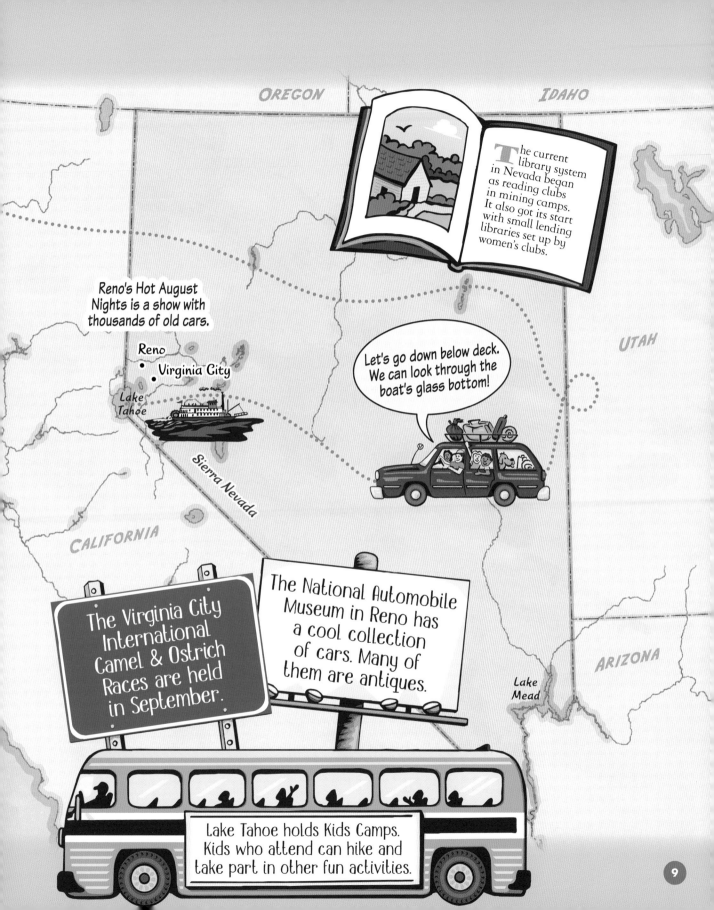

OREGON

IDAHO

The current library system in Nevada began as reading clubs in mining camps. It also got its start with small lending libraries set up by women's clubs.

UTAH

Reno's Hot August Nights is a show with thousands of old cars.

Reno
• Virginia City

Let's go down below deck. We can look through the boat's glass bottom!

Lake Tahoe

Sierra Nevada

CALIFORNIA

ARIZONA

Lake Mead

The Virginia City International Camel & Ostrich Races are held in September.

The National Automobile Museum in Reno has a cool collection of cars. Many of them are antiques.

Lake Tahoe holds Kids Camps. Kids who attend can hike and take part in other fun activities.

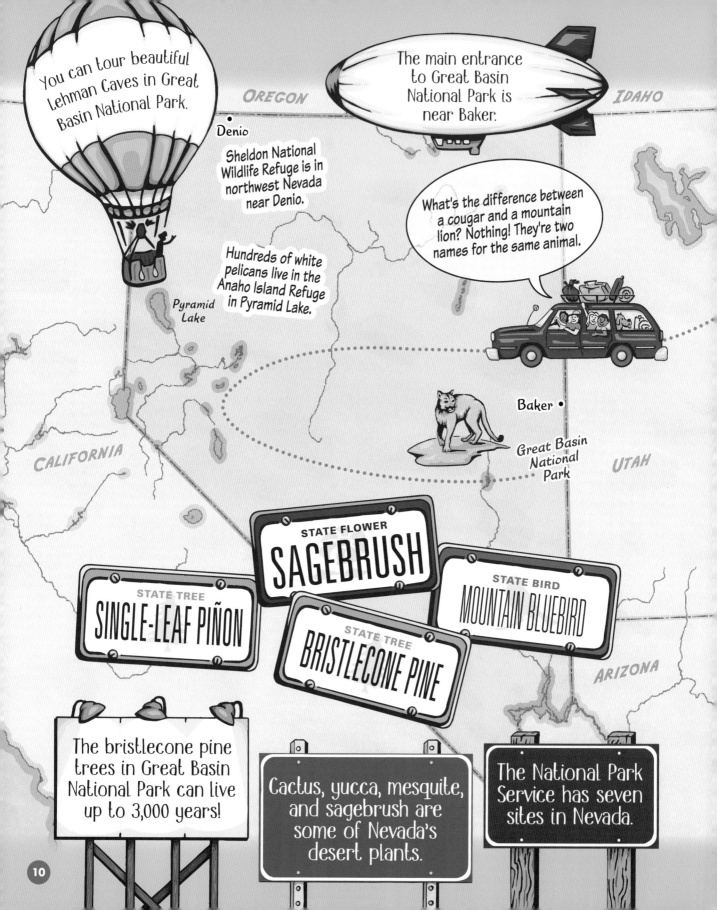

Nevada has many land features. Each one is home to special animals. Great Basin National Park is fun to explore. It has both dry deserts and lush mountains. Many different kinds of animals live there.

Sagebrush grows in the park's desert areas. Here, jackrabbits and ground squirrels scurry along the ground. Pronghorn antelopes run swiftly across the plains.

Pine and juniper trees grow on higher ground. There you'll find mule deer. Near streams, you'll see weasels and ringtail cats.

Mountain lions live on the rugged mountain slopes. You might see bighorn sheep and mountain goats, too. They're expert rock climbers!

Great Basin National Park has high mountains, thick forests, and clear waters.

EXPLORING THE RUBY MOUNTAINS

Many people think of Nevada as desert land. But they've never seen the Ruby Mountains!

These lush mountains are southeast of Elko. Their snowcapped peaks rise over green meadows. Sparkling blue lakes nestle in high valleys. Melting snow fills up the swift streams. The water rushes down the mountainsides.

Would you like to go hiking here? If you go, you'll meet lots of wildlife. Beavers, coyotes, and mule deer roam the forests. Mountain goats and bighorn sheep live here, too. You might see skunks or porcupines waddling along. Watch out! Don't get too close to either type of animal!

Skiers prepare to descend the Ruby Mountain slopes.

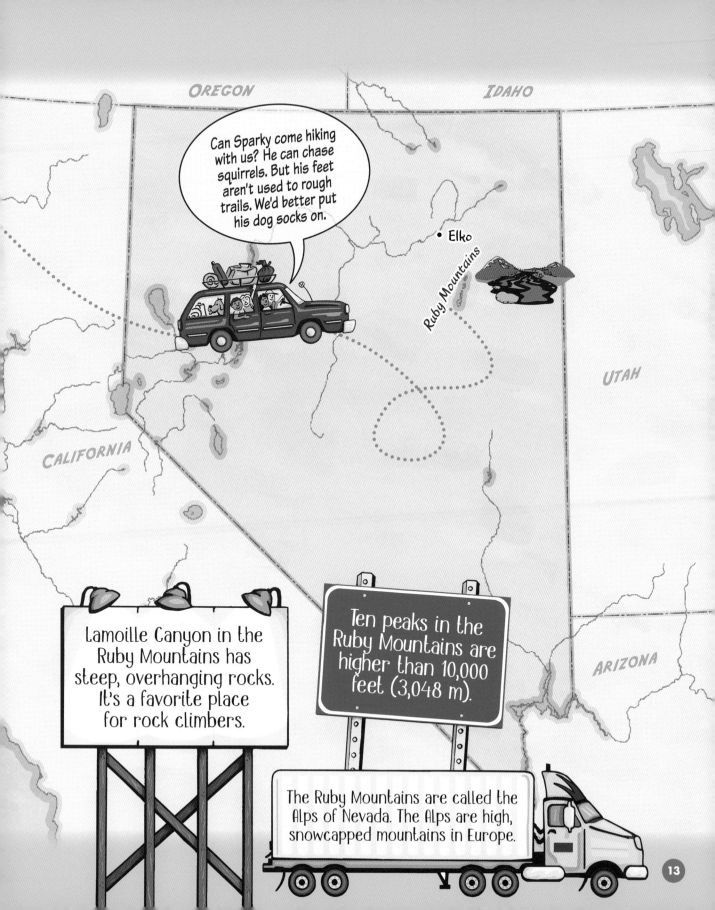

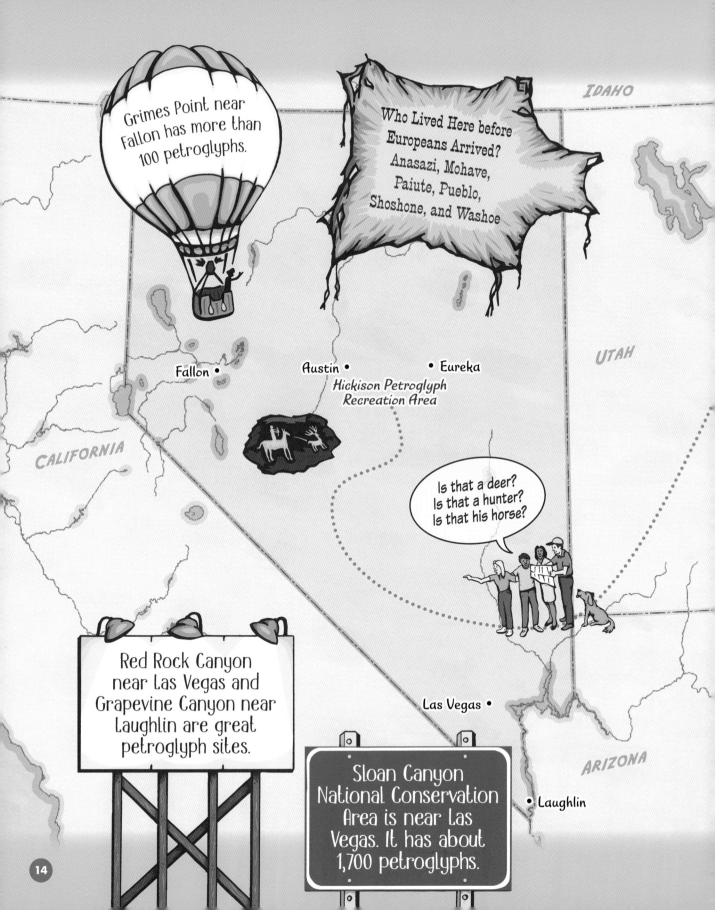

Grimes Point near Fallon has more than 100 petroglyphs.

Who Lived Here before Europeans Arrived?
Anasazi, Mohave, Paiute, Pueblo, Shoshone, and Washoe

IDAHO

UTAH

Fallon •

Austin •

• Eureka

Hickison Petroglyph Recreation Area

CALIFORNIA

Is that a deer?
Is that a hunter?
Is that his horse?

Red Rock Canyon near Las Vegas and Grapevine Canyon near Laughlin are great petroglyph sites.

Las Vegas •

Sloan Canyon National Conservation Area is near Las Vegas. It has about 1,700 petroglyphs.

ARIZONA

• Laughlin

PETROGLYPHS AT HICKISON PETROGLYPH RECREATION AREA

Head up the mountain at Hickison Petroglyph **Recreation** Area. It's about halfway between Austin and Eureka. Soon you'll see dozens of petroglyphs. Those are drawings carved into rock. Can you figure out what the pictures are?

Ancient people carved these drawings. They could be scenes of hunting activities. Nevada has many other petroglyph sites. Native Americans have lived in Nevada for thousands of years. Historians believe many of Hickison Point's petroglyphs were created by the Western Shoshone Native Americans. They think the Western Shoshone were the only people that lived in this area until the 1800s. That's when European explorers started heading west.

Today, Nevada has 32 Native American reservations. Four major tribes call Nevada home. They are the Washoe, Northern Paiute, Southern Paiute, and Western Shoshone.

These petroglyphs came from Grapevine Canyon in southern Nevada.

Visit a town that's filled with shops, outdoor activities, history, and art exhibits. It's Carson City!

In Carson City, you'll find antique shops lining the streets and local artists selling their crafts. Once you're done shopping, take a hike on one of the city's many trails. Different paths will lead you along the Carson River, to waterfalls, and to an elevated view of the city.

You can learn more about Nevada's history at the Nevada State Museum. Once you're done exploring the museum, take a historic ride on the city's train and watch the Nevada landscape fly by the window. There's so much to do in Carson City!

The historic Virginia & Truckee Railroad will take Carson City visitors to Virginia City.

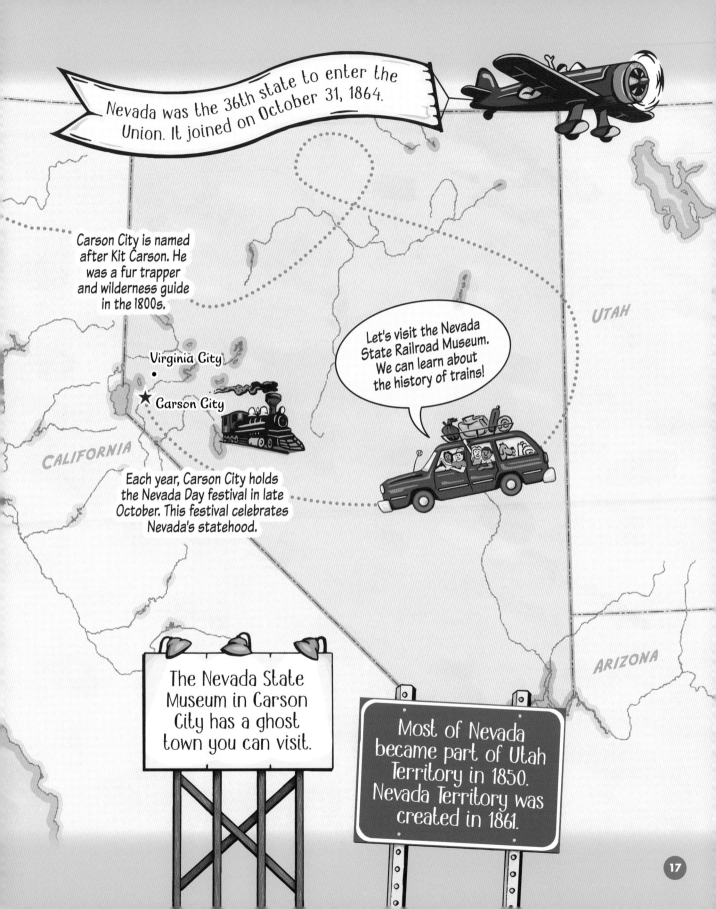

Nevada was the 36th state to enter the Union. It joined on October 31, 1864.

Carson City is named after Kit Carson. He was a fur trapper and wilderness guide in the 1800s.

Virginia City
★ Carson City

Let's visit the Nevada State Railroad Museum. We can learn about the history of trains!

Each year, Carson City holds the Nevada Day festival in late October. This festival celebrates Nevada's statehood.

CALIFORNIA

UTAH

ARIZONA

The Nevada State Museum in Carson City has a ghost town you can visit.

Most of Nevada became part of Utah Territory in 1850. Nevada Territory was created in 1861.

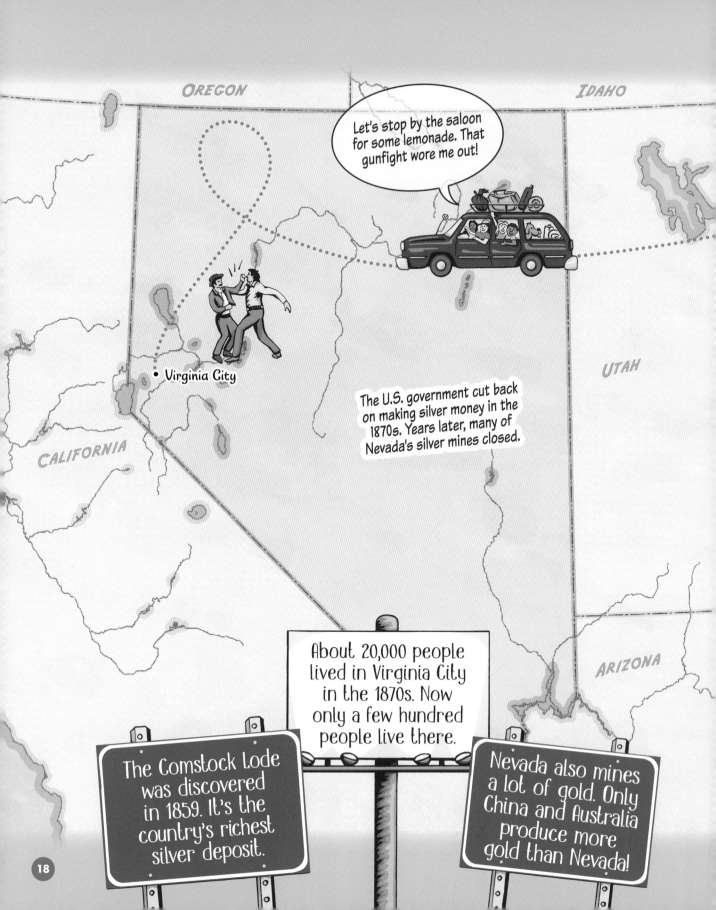

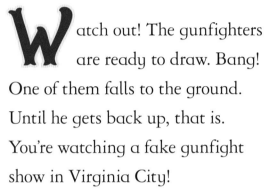

HOT TIMES IN VIRGINIA CITY

Watch out! The gunfighters are ready to draw. Bang! One of them falls to the ground. Until he gets back up, that is. You're watching a fake gunfight show in Virginia City!

Virginia City was once a pretty wild town. A huge deposit of silver was found nearby. It was called the Comstock **Lode**. Gold was found in Virginia City, too.

Thousands of people rushed in to get rich. Wild, lawless mining camps sprang up. People were rowdy and got into fights. A few people made big fortunes. But most found nothing and didn't stay. The towns they left became **ghost towns**.

Today, Virginia City has many spots to shop.

THE WILD BURRO RANGE IN MARIETTA

Want to see herds of wild, free-roaming burros? Just head out to the Wild Burro Range in Marietta! More than 80 wild burros live there.

A burro is a small donkey. Burros were useful in the Old West. They were used as pack animals. They are sure-footed on mountainous land.

Miners brought burros

here in the late 1800s. The miners were looking for silver and gold. Some of the burros escaped. They had babies. Soon there was a big herd of wild burros!

Miners would use burros to carry their things when searching for gold and silver.

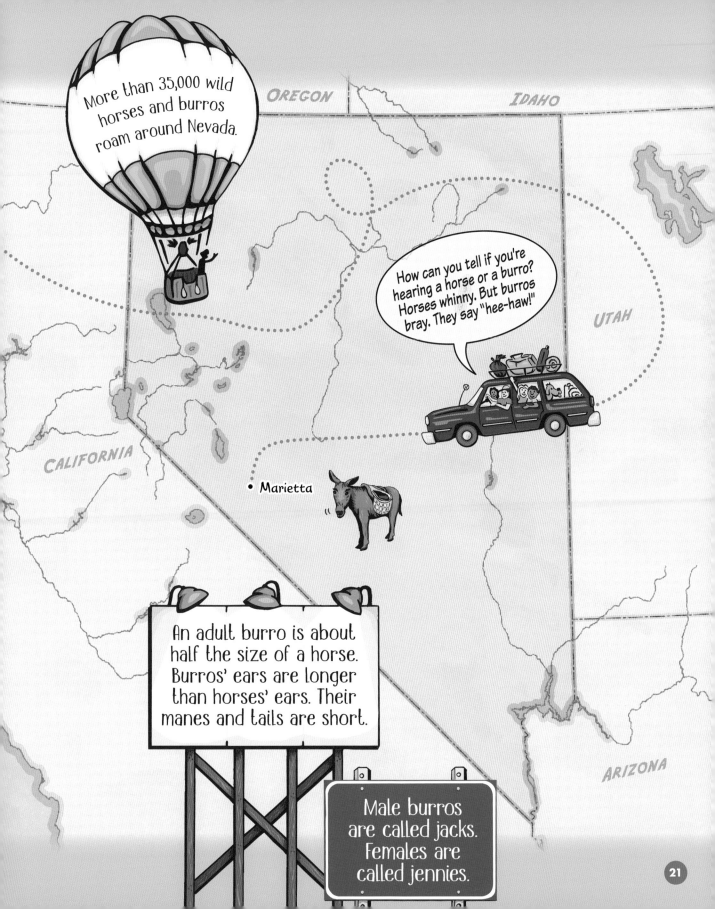

More than 35,000 wild horses and burros roam around Nevada.

OREGON

IDAHO

How can you tell if you're hearing a horse or a burro? Horses whinny. But burros bray. They say "hee-haw!"

UTAH

CALIFORNIA

• Marietta

An adult burro is about half the size of a horse. Burros' ears are longer than horses' ears. Their manes and tails are short.

Male burros are called jacks. Females are called jennies.

ARIZONA

About 94 out of 100 Nevadans live in cities or towns as opposed to rural areas.

Let's find a good spot on the street to watch the parade!

Elko

In 2016, 2,904,058 people lived in Nevada. It's the 34th-largest state by population.

Reno •

CALIFORNIA

UTAH

The Western Folklife Center is in Elko. It's a place to explore Nevada's Western culture.

Population of Largest Cities

Las Vegas	623,769
Henderson	285,658
Reno	241,443

ARIZONA

Las Vegas
•
• Henderson

Many Basques had been sheepherders. They kept up this skill in the United States.

Euskara is the native language of the Basque people.

Reno also holds a Basque festival every summer.

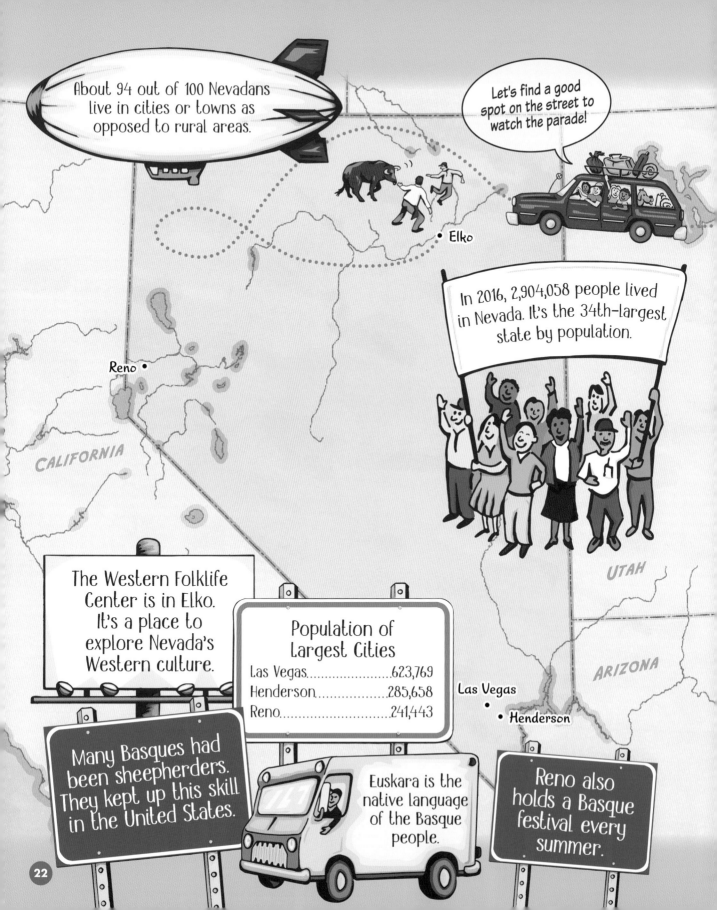

ELKO'S NATIONAL BASQUE FESTIVAL

Every year, people gather in Elko to eat food, listen to music, dance, and have a great time! Since 1964, Elko has held a National Basque Festival. The festival started as a celebration that brought cattle ranchers and sheepherders into town.

Stick around for the weekend-long event. You'll see weight-lifting and wood-chopping contests. People will be dancing in colorful costumes, too.

Basque **immigrants** arrived in California in the 1800s. They came from the mountainous Basque Region. It crosses the border between Spain and France. From California, they moved into Nevada. Their **descendants** still love to celebrate their **traditions**!

Stop by and watch the dancers at the Basque Festival.

THE STATE CAPITOL IN CARSON CITY

Nevada's state capitol in Carson City is pretty old. State leaders began meeting there in 1871. This building is the center of state government.

Nevada's government has three branches. One branch consists of the state lawmakers. Another branch carries out the laws. The governor heads this branch. Judges make up the third branch. They decide whether laws have been broken.

Many newer buildings surround the capitol. The lawmakers meet in one building. The state's highest court meets in another. Only the governor's offices remain in the capitol.

The governor's offices are in Carson City's capitol building.

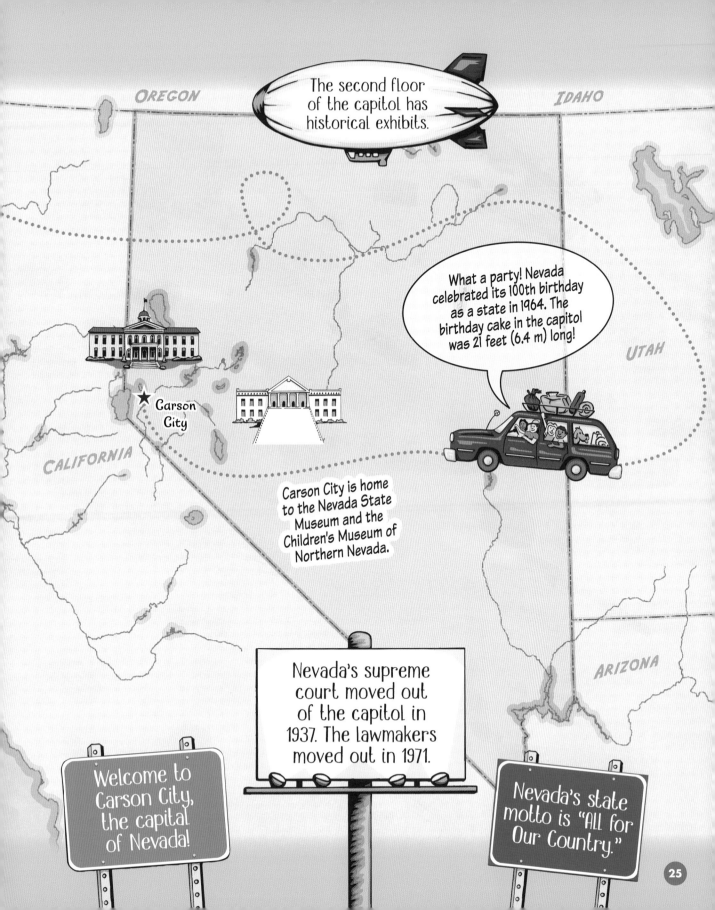

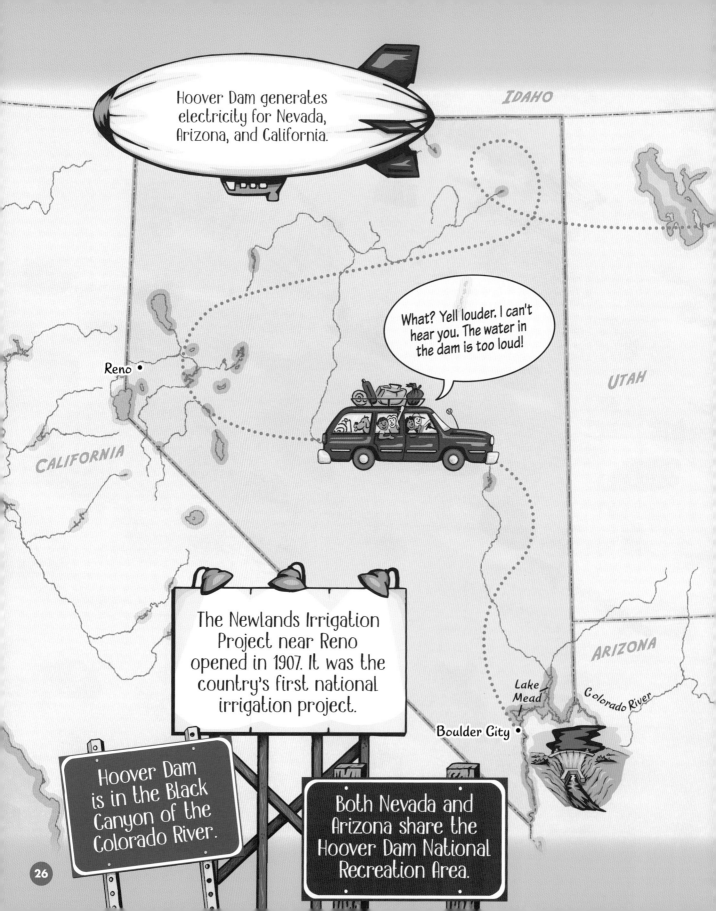

Hoover Dam generates electricity for Nevada, Arizona, and California.

IDAHO

What? Yell louder. I can't hear you. The water in the dam is too loud!

UTAH

Reno •

CALIFORNIA

The Newlands Irrigation Project near Reno opened in 1907. It was the country's first national irrigation project.

ARIZONA

Lake Mead

Colorado River

Boulder City •

Hoover Dam is in the Black Canyon of the Colorado River.

Both Nevada and Arizona share the Hoover Dam National Recreation Area.

VISITING HOOVER DAM

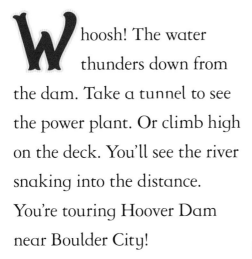

Whoosh! The water thunders down from the dam. Take a tunnel to see the power plant. Or climb high on the deck. You'll see the river snaking into the distance. You're touring Hoover Dam near Boulder City!

Hoover Dam is one of Nevada's water projects. Many were built in the early 1900s. They all involve dams across rivers.

The dams have many benefits. They control floods and store water for **irrigation**. Some create lakes. Many dams provide **hydroelectric** power, too. Hoover Dam stretches across the Colorado River. It was completed in 1935. Lake Mead backs up behind the dam. It's a great recreation spot!

Hoover Dam is 726 feet (221 m) tall!

TOURING THE NEVADA NATIONAL SECURITY SITE

It looks like an endless desert. You see massive holes in the ground. You pass a house with broken-out windows.

You're touring the Nevada National Security Site. It covers a huge area northwest of Las Vegas. The U.S. government once tested **nuclear** weapons here.

The first test took place in 1951. A 1962 test created Sedan Crater. It's a huge hole made by explosives.

Nuclear tests stopped in 1992. Now the center does many kinds of studies. It tests rockets, weapons, and dangerous waste materials.

Nuclear weapons were once tested at the Nevada National Security Site.

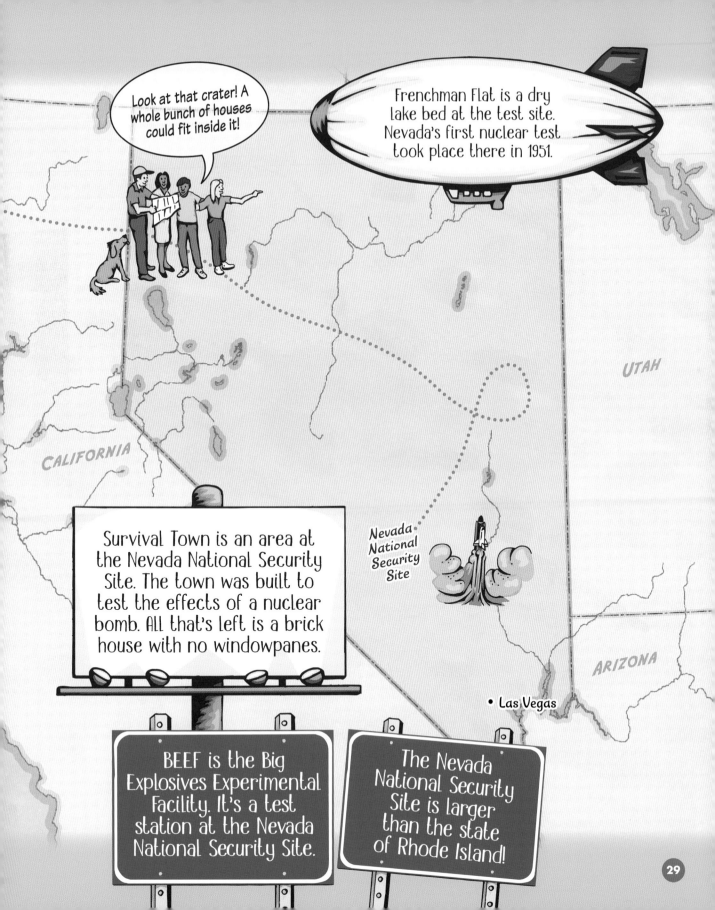

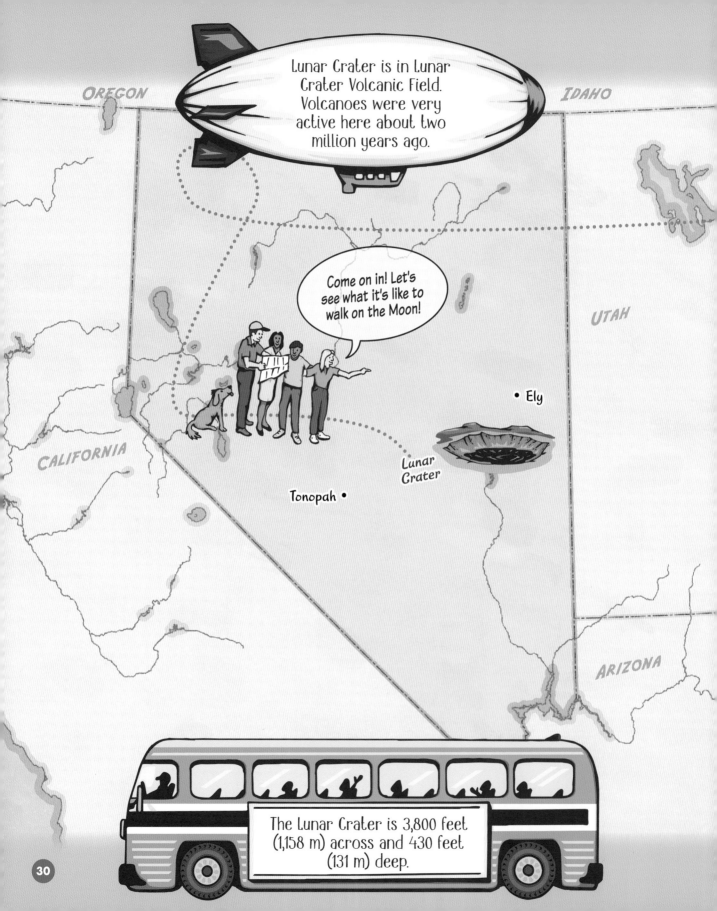

NEVADA'S LUNAR CRATER

Stand on the edge of the hole. It's more than 12 football fields wide! It looks like a giant **meteor** fell there. But it's actually where a volcano erupted. Then the volcano collapsed. That created the big hole. Now that hole is called the Lunar Crater! It's halfway between Ely and Tonopah.

What's a lunar crater? It's a bowl-shaped hole in the Moon's surface. Of course, this is not the Moon. But people thought the crater looked like the Moon.

The crater has a rough, rugged surface. In that way, it is like the Moon. Astronauts trained there in the 1960s. They were training to go to the Moon!

Lunar Crater is one of Nevada's six National Natural Landmarks.

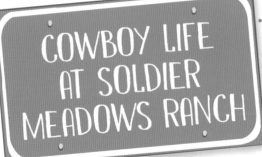

COWBOY LIFE AT SOLDIER MEADOWS RANCH

Want to live the cowboy life? Just spend some time at Soldier Meadows Ranch and Lodge. It's northeast of Gerlach. You can ride horses there. You can even work with the cowboys!

Ranching is the state's major farm activity. Nevada has many cattle and sheep ranches. These animals produce meat, milk, and wool. They have lots of grazing land in Nevada.

You'll find crops growing in the river valleys. Most crop farming is done with irrigation. In some areas, farmers pump water from underground. Hay is Nevada's top crop. And no wonder! The cattle need it for food.

Learn all about ranch life and see cattle at Soldier Meadows Ranch.

OREGON

IDAHO

• Gerlach

• Elko

Giddy-up, horsey! Let's ride out on the range. We might see herds of wild horses out there!

• Reno

UTAH

The state fair is held in Reno in August each year.

CALIFORNIA

The U.S. government owns most of Nevada's land. Ranchers pay a fee to graze their cattle on government-owned land.

Elko holds the National Cowboy Poetry Gathering every January.

ARIZONA

• Las Vegas

What Does Nevada Raise?
Beef cattle, hay, and sheep

Nevada's biggest rodeo is the National Finals Rodeo in Las Vegas every December.

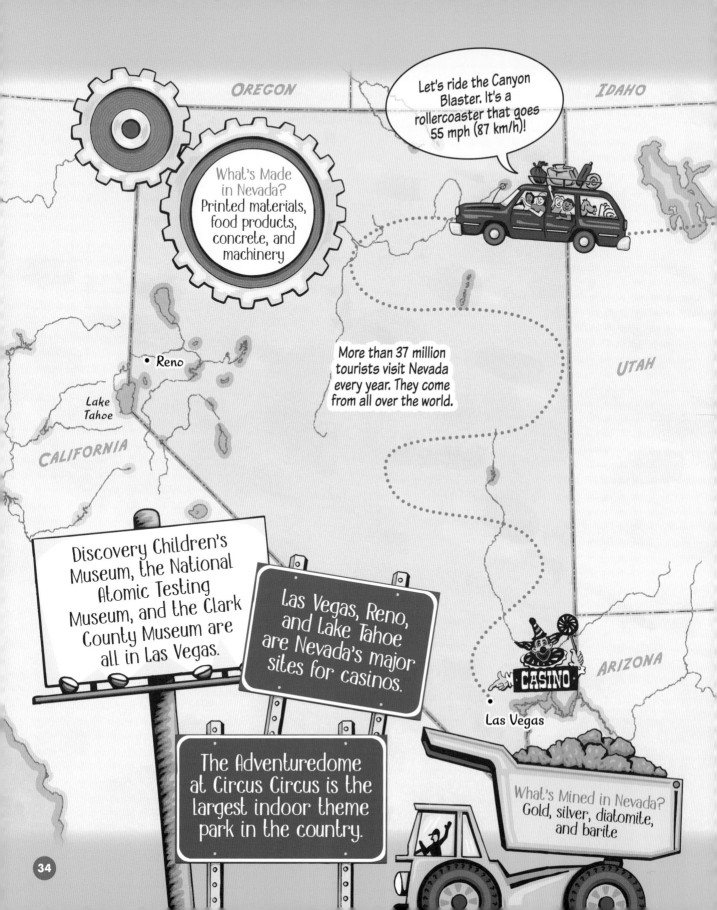

LAS VEGAS FOR KIDS!

Spend a day in the Adventuredome. You'll take thrilling roller coaster rides. You'll bang around in bumper cars. And you'll see clown acts and trapeze shows.

You're at Circus Circus! It's a big hotel in Las Vegas.

Tourism is Nevada's biggest industry. Many Nevada tourists come to Las Vegas. Grown-ups try to win money at **casinos** there. But Las Vegas has great places for kids, too.

Mandalay Bay is another fun hotel. You can walk through tunnels inside shark tanks. You'll really get close to the sharks! Eek!

The Adventuredome has 20 rides and attractions for visitors.

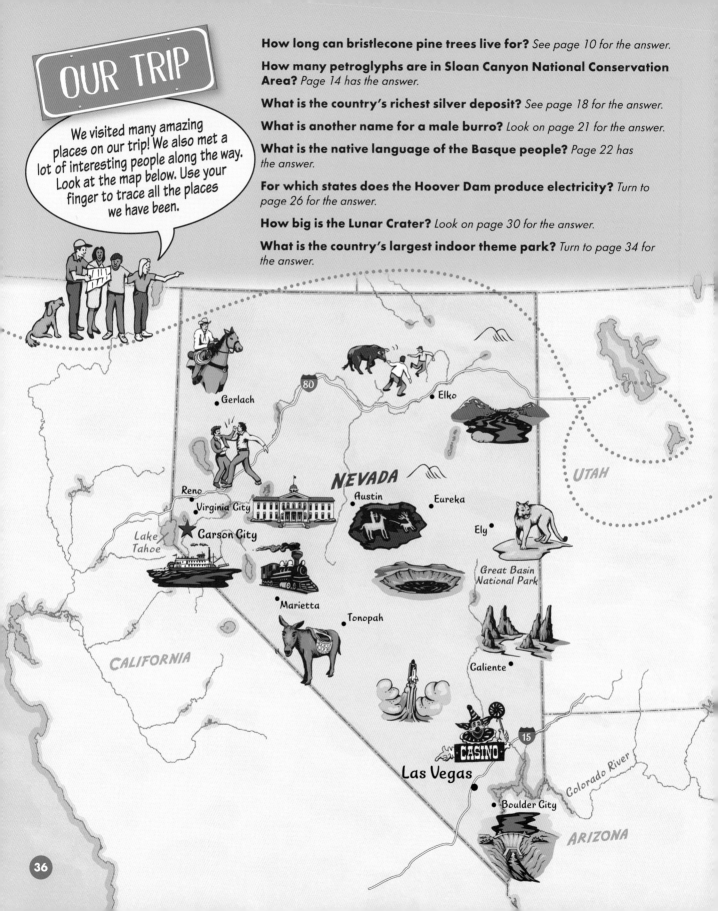

OUR TRIP

We visited many amazing places on our trip! We also met a lot of interesting people along the way. Look at the map below. Use your finger to trace all the places we have been.

How long can bristlecone pine trees live for? *See page 10 for the answer.*

How many petroglyphs are in Sloan Canyon National Conservation Area? *Page 14 has the answer.*

What is the country's richest silver deposit? *See page 18 for the answer.*

What is another name for a male burro? *Look on page 21 for the answer.*

What is the native language of the Basque people? *Page 22 has the answer.*

For which states does the Hoover Dam produce electricity? *Turn to page 26 for the answer.*

How big is the Lunar Crater? *Look on page 30 for the answer.*

What is the country's largest indoor theme park? *Turn to page 34 for the answer.*

STATE SYMBOLS

State animal: Desert bighorn sheep

State artifact: Tule duck decoy

State bird: Mountain bluebird

State fish: Lahontan cutthroat trout

State flower: Sagebrush

State fossil: Ichthyosaur

State grass: Indian rice grass

State metal: Silver

State precious gemstone:
Virgin Valley black fire opal

State reptile: Desert tortoise

State rock: Sandstone

State semiprecious gemstone:
Nevada turquoise

State trees: Single-leaf piñon
and bristlecone pine

STATE SONG

"HOME MEANS NEVADA"
Words and music by Bertha Raffetto

Way out in the land of the
  setting sun,
Where the wind blows wild
  and free,
There's a lovely spot, just the
  only one
That means home sweet home
  to me.
If you follow the old Kit
  Carson trail,
Until desert meets the hills,
Oh you certainly will agree
  with me,
It's the place of a thousand thrills.

Chorus:
Home means Nevada,
Home means the hills,
Home means the sage and
  the pines.
Out by the Truckee's silvery rills,
Out where the Sun always shines,

There is the land that I love
  the best,
Fairer than all I can see.
Right in the heart of the
  golden west
Home means Nevada to me.

Whenever the sun at the close
  of day,
Colors all the western sky,
Oh my heart returns to the
  desert grey
And the mountains tow'ring high.
Where the moon beams play in
  shadowed glen,
With the spotted fawn and doe,
All the livelong night until
  morning light,
Is the loveliest place I know.

(Chorus)

That was a great trip! We have traveled all over Nevada! There are a few places we didn't have time for, though. Next time, we plan to visit the Fleischmann Planetarium and Science Center in Reno. Visitors can watch star shows and use telescopes. The center also features a large meteorite collection.

State flag

State seal

FAMOUS PEOPLE

Agassi, Andre (1970–), tennis player

Ashurst, Henry Fountain (1874–1962), politician

Bentley, Helen Delich (1923–2016), journalist and politician

Bilbray, James Hubert (1938–), politician

Busch, Kyle (1985–), professional car racing driver

Casey, James E. (1888–1983), founder of the United Parcel Service (UPS)

Clark, Walter van Tilburg (1909–1971), author

Dat-So-La-Lee (ca. 1829–1925), Washoe Native American basket weaver

Gubler, Matthew Gray (1980–), actor, director

Harper, Bryce (1992–), baseball player

Kramer, Jack (1921–2009), tennis player

Laxalt, Paul (1922–), former governor of Nevada

Laxalt, Robert (1923–2001), author

Maddux, Greg (1966–), baseball player

Malone, Jena (1984–), actress, musician

Nixon, Pat (1912–1993), former first lady of the United States

Purviance, Edna (1895–1958), actor

Reid, Harry M. (1939–), politician

Winnemucca, Sarah (ca. 1844–1891), Northern Paiute Native American author and reformer

Wovoka (ca. 1856–1932), Paiute Native American religious leader

Zajick, Dolora (1952–), opera singer

WORDS TO KNOW

casinos (kuh-SEE-noze) places where people play games of chance to win money

descendants (de-SEND-dants) people who are ancestors of a particular group

ghost towns (GOHST TOWNZ) towns that are empty because everyone has moved away

hydroelectric (hye-droh-i-LEK-trik) relating to electric energy produced by water power

immigrants (IM-uh-gruhnts) people who leave their home country and move to another country

irrigation (eer-uh-GAY-shuhn) bringing water to fields through ditches or pipes

lode (LOHD) a deposit of rock that contains valuable metals

meteor (MEE-tee-ur) a rock that falls from space

nuclear (NOO-klee-ur) relating to the energy produced by splitting atoms

recreation (rek-ree-AY-shuhn) games, sports, or hobbies that people enjoy in their spare time

traditions (truh-DISH-uhnz) long-held customs

tram (TRAM) a boxlike car that travels on overhead wires

TO LEARN MORE

IN THE LIBRARY

Felix, Rebecca. *What's Great About Nevada?* Minneapolis, MN: Lerner, 2016.

Goldish, Meish. *The Hoover Dam.* New York, NY: Bearport Publishing, 2017.

Hoena, Blake. *Nevada: The Battle Born State.* Minneapolis, MN: Bellwether, 2014.

Miller, Heather. *The Hoover Dam (Great Idea).* Chicago, IL: Norwood House, 2014.

ON THE WEB

Visit our Web site for links about Nevada:
childsworld.com/links

Note to Parents, Teachers, and Librarians: We routinely verify our Web links to make sure they are safe and active sites. So encourage your readers to check them out!

PLACES TO VISIT OR CONTACT

Nevada Historical Society
nvdtca.org/historicalsociety
1650 North Virginia Street
Reno, NV 89503
775/688-1190
For more information about the history of Nevada

Travel Nevada
travelnevada.com
401 North Carson Street
Carson City, NV 89701
800/638-2328
For more information about traveling in Nevada

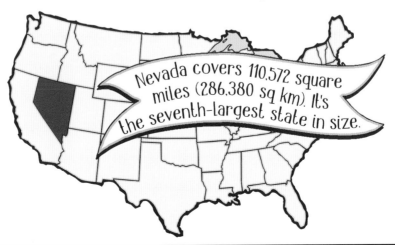

Nevada covers 110,572 square miles (286,380 sq km). It's the seventh-largest state in size.

INDEX

Bye, Silver State. We had a great time. We'll come back soon!